Greenhouse Garden

For Beginners

Contents

INTRODUCTION

Greenhouse gardening is not a contemporary idea. The technology and system date back to the Roman Realm. The earliest reference to the greenhouse gardening concept is directed to the Roman Emperor Tiberius. He demanded to have Armenian cucumbers every day at the royal table. Royal gardeners thought of ways to obey the emperor's order. They found out that by creating a sealed enclosure, they can control temperatures, humidity, and light exposure required by cucumbers for growth and fruit-bearing. They used a special system very similar to that of modern greenhouses.

During those times, having a greenhouse was limited to the wealthy. By the 19th century, greenhouses became more of an academic need. Universities put up large greenhouses, designed to hold several rare species of plants. During this time, Western civilization was starting to explore the other side of the world. Explorers and scholars were bringing back a lot of specimens from these exotic places, most of which were pretty interesting, but cannot tolerate cold climates. In order to preserve the plants in their full, natural bloom, greenhouses were the likely solution.

Greenhouse gardening can then be defined as the discipline of growing plants in a founded building through materials typically translucent or transparent. The plants are provided with controlled favorable environmental conditions. Plants that are cultivated in greenhouses receive protection against conditions like soil erosion, harsh weather, violent rain and storm, plant pathogens, etc. This gardening system is also called glasshouse or hothouse by some growers. The major reason for setting it up is probably to secure a considerable quantity of water vapor and heat to maintain humidity and proper temperature in the greenhouse.

The technology of greenhouse gardening serves as a viable solution to bridge the gap between the increasing world population and the increasing demand. The gap was created due to the urbanization of certain countries involving the construction of roads, etc., and industrialization, which has inevitably made much arable land uncultivable.

The growth of plants under adverse weather conditions will eventually become stunted, this is why plants grow better in a greenhouse, although the growth of plants in the greenhouse is influenced by humidity, ventilation, light, and also the rate of plant watering. The environmental condition of the greenhouse can be classified into the physical environment—which includes water, light, temperature, etc.—and the biotic environment—which includes insects, microorganisms, etc. Humidity levels above 85% in the greenhouse should, by all means, be avoided as this tends to cause more harm than good to the plants. When the humidity level in the greenhouse is too much, the plants become weak and flaccid, in which case the humid air needs to be exhausted. The need for the presence of fresh air in the greenhouse cannot be overemphasized as it encourages photosynthesis, pollination, and pest prevention. Plants generally require about 6–12 hours of light daily, therefore, in a situation where the plants in the greenhouse are not exposed to enough natural light, artificial light should be incorporated and adequately so. Also, too much supply of water in the greenhouse is just as dangerous to the plants as the lack of water supply. But factors such as growing medium, temperature, plant size, etc. contribute greatly to the determination of the amount of watering required by the plant. After you have selected the location to set up your greenhouse, the building can be self-built by placing an order for an already made "Do-It-Yourself" greenhouse kit. Setting things up in most cases is simple but in some other cases, it can also be a bit complex. For starters, not much high-tech equipment is required to practice greenhouse gardening. The greenhouse technique can be practiced simply or expanded depending on the scale of production intended.

Gardening in Ancient Times

Our story begins with one of the oldest known countries in the world, Egypt. When people hear the name Egypt, they usually think of the Great Pyramid at Giza, or perhaps the legendary Sphinx and its riddles. They might also think of the pharaohs, the great kings and champions of Egypt; others might remember the boy king named Tutankhamen. However, aside from its great pyramids and its plethora of gods and goddesses, Egypt has another contribution to the world's shared culture.
Around 4000 B.C., the Egyptians mastered the planting and harvesting of grapes. There are tomb drawings and hieroglyphs (ancient Egyptian writing) that show Egyptian farmers in the act of cutting grapes from vines, or sowing grape seeds in the soil. The Egyptians, like many nations around the world, knew that settled communities had to have a reliable source of food. No community, large or small, could hunt all the prey in the wild without bringing about a great disaster. So, all around the world, nations turned to the earth, wind, rain, and sun for the miracle of plant life.
The Egyptians were just one of the countries that figured out how to use seeds and plants as a food source. In China, some of the great scholars of the emperor prescribed certain ceremonies for sowing and planting seeds. This is reminiscent of tribal practices, like the dance of the Native American Indians during a good harvest.

On another distant shore, the Greeks were marveling at the life that sprouted from the ground. Their philosophers began asking questions about the origin and meaning of life. The natural sciences soon began to take hold in Greece. Around 300 B.C., Plato mentioned a few vague hints about "protected cultivation" in some of his writings. Later, during the same period, another intellectual, by the name of Theophrastus, observed that plots with manure mixed in them seemed riper and richer than those that had none. Theophrastus also mentioned that the ripened soil appeared to make the crops grow faster and healthier.

In Italy, many inventions were taking the country by storm. A man named Sergius Orata discovered how to make a heating system that passed heat through flues or vents in the floor. Other notable Italians like Columella and Pliny wrote about the use of different materials to protect young plants from harsh sunlight, excessive wind, and flood. During 100 to 380 A.D., the Italians were slowly learning how to manipulate the environment of plants to ensure their safety and fruitfulness.

Gardening in the Early Centuries (12th to 16th Century)

During the time of the Crusades, the Crusaders themselves helped spread a variety of plants by carrying them from their place of origin to foreign soil. Of course, for people who had never seen orchids or strange-shaped plants and herbs, these exotic treasures had to be replicated for the entire nation to enjoy. This started the plant trade and the endeavors of gardeners all around the world to successfully grow beautiful plants even though they were not suited to the country's climate.

In 1385 a story about flowers being grown in a glass pavilion in France captivated many gardeners. They, too, wanted to know what the glass pavilion was for, and whether or not they would be able to have their own. The story goes that the pavilion was built facing the south of France, for the plants to better catch the warm breeze during the day and be shielded from harsh wind.

Finally, during the Renaissance, reports of sheds with heating vents in them became the new standard for the middle class. During the 16th century, the green glass industry in Italy flourished. In the year 1550, the first botanical garden with a greenhouse was built at Padua.

The Greenhouse and Gardening in the 21st Century

The idea of having a place in which plants and flowers can bloom all year-round is a gardener's vision of paradise. Thus, when the glass industry boomed, and the idea for using better soil as well as heat manipulation for planting first came about in earlier centuries, the destiny of the greenhouse was already cast in stone. For many gardeners, having their own greenhouses right across their homes is indeed a dream come true. Instead of having to wait for the seasons to change, or for winter to pass, the gardeners can cultivate different kinds of fauna in the same enclosed space.

Today, with the rise of organic gardening, aquaponics, and other agriculture or aquaculture-related practices, the greenhouse stands at its prime. More and more individuals have returned to the basic necessities so highly valued by our ancestors: good food, and a healthy relationship with the earth, and elements that give birth to our sustenance.

So, you see, engaging in greenhouse gardening is not only about having a separate space in which to grow rare plants. It is also about connecting with nature on a deeper level and engaging in an activity so rewarding; you will never want to stop. The practice of greenhouse gardening offers many opportunities to anyone with a budding green thumb.

DIFFERENT TYPES OF GREENHOUSES

Greenhouses make it possible for gardeners to increase their growth opportunities. Plants that struggle to bear fruit outdoors might produce fantastic yields under the glass. Vegetables growing wouldn't be limited by seasons. Before you begin growing plants in a greenhouse, it's ideal to decide the type of construction that will meet your needs. Consider the available space, light exposure, utility hookups, and the cost. Here are some of the structures to consider when choosing a greenhouse of choice:

Lean-To Greenhouses

Attached or lean-to greenhouses are less expensive and an excellent choice with limited space. This type of greenhouse shares one wall with your house, garage or other structure. Lean-to has available utility sources close by and is economical to manage than a freestanding greenhouse. It also has the advantages of having a wall on which to nurture ornamental climbers or fruit. Also, it offers better heat retention if the wall is brick. However, the height of the shared wall will limit its potential size. The transparent greenhouse cover and solid wall might be at odds, with the wall receiving the sunlight while the roof loses it quickly. A bigger type of a lean-to is a full-size construction that attached to a building. Apart from offering more ample space, it has a better shape for ventilation.

Window-Mounted Greenhouses

Window-mounted is the most economical and smallest type of greenhouses. They are attached to the outer window of the house, most importantly east or south side. The glass cover broadens a foot or more outward and may contain 2 or 3 shelves for growing a few plants. The significant challenge for a window-mounted greenhouse is keeping a uniform temperature. As its heat depends on the house's interior temperature, the purpose is to keep the plants warm enough without the house being overheated.

Freestanding Greenhouses

Freestanding greenhouses as the name implies, are separate structures. There are many options for size and provision must be made for water, heat, and electricity. The bigger greenhouses are more convenient to manage because the temperature of the smaller ones fluctuates more rapidly. After you must choose materials for the frame and cover, the next thing to decide is the frame's shape. With a freestanding greenhouse, you will have the opportunity to start planting earlier in the growing season and then, when frost begins, you may take your plants inside to extend the season.

Quonset Greenhouse

A Quonset greenhouse is vault molded and provides a perfect entrance for sunlight. These structures have warming frameworks, aeration frameworks, dissemination fans, and enhanced innate control. The leeway of this type of greenhouse is that they work very well on slopes and increases warming from the sunlight. The disadvantage of it is that they're expensive and require more assistance because of the uneven structure.

A greenhouse is what most gardeners wish for, as it enables you to grow plants all year round irrespective of the weather. Nevertheless, the above structures may be pricey; as a result, you may want to opt for less expensive materials and structure. Greenhouses require very similar basic features that will allow you to be innovative in building your own by opting for cheaper conventional materials. The cost can also be reduced by making use of recycled materials to construct your greenhouse. Here are some cheap and simple materials to construct your greenhouses:

Old Window Structure

Glass is usually very costly, but making use of recycled sources of glass would lessen your expenses. For example, you can use old windows to build a greenhouse. With this type of  greenhouse, you will make the walls from the old windows that are connected, either you attach the frames together, or you attach them to a wooden structure. It will result in an interesting and attracting aesthetics effect, though the method needs planning and a little carpentry skill, especially if your windows are of different sizes. Note: Do not use windows for the roof; instead make use of different material like transparent plastic roofing sheet.

Wooden Cold Frames

Cold frames are structures often constructed with greenhouses and are generally used to acclimate seedlings to the cooler air outside the building. Making an economic cold frame for your greenhouse is simple. A conventional cold frame only needs a wooden frame with a slanting top and an old window to cover the top as a lid. A hinge can be added to the rear of the box to connect to the lid, and this will make open and close easier. Additionally, polycarbonate plastic sheets can be used in place of glass as it won't break.

USES AND BENEFITS OF GREENHOUSE GARDENING

Whether gardening is your hobby or profession, building a greenhouse can take your efforts to the next level. It can also save you from the drastic consequences caused by unpredictable weather.

The primary purpose of greenhouse gardening is to protect crops from extreme weather conditions (both in the summer and winter) and pesky pests. The glasshouse shields it from environmental elements to promote the healthy growth of all types of plants, including ones you won't necessarily find in your region.

Here's a closer look at all the reasons why you should build a greenhouse:

Optimum Planting

Unpredictable can wash away or flood your backyard overnight. Even if the consequences are not severe, continuous storms and fluctuating temperatures can have a negative impact on plant growth. Without proper intervention, it can lead to ruined vegetable patches and rotten fruits.

Fortunately, a greenhouse can save you from potential heartbreaks and ruined crops. These weather-proof structures evade unfavorable seasonal changes by regulating the internal environment. Consistent temperature and humidity ensure that your plants grow without disruptions.

Consequently, your gardening efforts are no longer dependent on the natural environment. Eliminating this connection paves the way for versatility, and experimentation. Hobbyists and professionals can use greenhouses to adopt new gardening styles and diversify their planting options.

You Get to Grow More Plants

Greenhouses create sufficient insulation and heat for warm-season plants to survive regardless of their location. They are also more humid and warmer than the natural outdoor environment. These factors make the hothouses excellent choices for growing tropical plants (i.e., cranberry hibiscus, bananas, ginger, pineapple, papaya, and more) in colder regions.

What's more? There are no hard and fast rules about the type of plants you need to grow inside a glasshouse. The flexibility allows you to create the glass structure into a multipurpose gardening zone. The possibilities are endless here.

Some gardeners switch things by growing indoor and outdoor plant varieties under one roof. Depending on individual gardening requirements, you can also use a mix of potted plants and plants directly grown on your soil.

If you plan things strategically, you can designate a section for fruits, vegetables, herbs, tobacco plants, and much more. The variety itself will make you feel giddy with excitement as you undertake an exceptional range of planting projects.

Enjoy a Year-Round Harvest

Gardeners have to follow a strict schedule when they are gardening in the open. Many plants have specific harvest cycles that you need to maintain dutifully. The stakes are higher for seasonal plants. All this can take a toll on you and also make it more challenging to get a good harvest each year.

Greenhouses lift off these restrictions by extending the growing season. With its assistance, you can grow plants a few weeks (and sometimes months) longer than expected. All thanks to its well-regulated and weather-proof environment.

Keep Pesky Pests Away

Backyards are open invitations for pests, critters, and animals lingering around the neighborhood like any grassy area. These trespassers have no qualms about biting into your juicing fruits and veggies or walking all over the vegetable patch, squashing everything in their wake.

Worse than one-time invaders are the pests that start living inside your yard. These critters can become difficult to detect when they first drop by. They can also breed and multiply within weeks. These variables make it impossible for you to manage pests without causing problems for your beautiful garden.

Plus, most pest prevention techniques are invasive or toxic. Frequent usage can affect plant growth and trigger unwanted plant diseases.

You can prevent this from happening by building a greenhouse for your garden. The sturdy structure will function as an extra barrier against unwanted pests and critters. It also minimizes the use of toxic pesticides in the long-run.

Cost-Effective Investment

If you think greenhouses are costly investments, we have news for you. These hothouses are so much more than a 'gardening accessory.' Not only do greenhouses save your plants, but they prevent unwanted gardening expenses too. Imagine how much maintenance costs and repair fees you will have to pay without this protection. When you think about it, these advantages reduce your gardening budget too.

Greenhouses also generate greater yields for seasonal and non-seasonal fruit. The increase in production rates means more revenue for your small-scale gardening business. If you do not sell your fruits and vegetables, you still save a lot by skipping grocery runs for fresh produce.

In addition to this, greenhouses are multifunctional. They have enough storage space for your gardening tools. These might include small items like shovels, shears, and spare pots to bigger tools such as lawnmowers. Having a greenhouse eliminates the need to manage additional expenses required for building or expanding a garden shed. You also save storage space in your garages and basements.

Here are a lot of considerations to be made before you get started a greenhouse. Obviously, there is a budget, but other factors may well influence your budget. If you live in a particularly cold area, double glazing and heating are important, but the primary considerations would be airflow and ventilation in a hotter area.

What Size to Buy

Bigger is not always best, but many people aspire to a large greenhouse. What size to buy will depend on the space you have available plus what you are planning to grow. Of course, no matter what size you buy, when you start to use it, you will run out of space and wish you'd bought a bigger one!

If you are buying a second-hand greenhouse or picking one up for free, then you have less choice in size and will usually make do with whatever comes up.

The most common size is 8x6-inch though you can get slightly smaller ones and very much larger ones. This is a good starter size, but you need to be aware that your space is limited, and you will struggle to fit a lot in. However, it is a great size for starting off seeds and growing a few tomatoes or chili plants.

Check any local planning or zoning regulations before you buy a greenhouse. If you are on an allotment, then check their rules too. The last thing you want is to put up your new greenhouse only to find you have breached a rule and then have to take it down. On allotments, you often need written permission for a greenhouse and to position it in a certain way. As to HOA's, their rules are anyone's guess, so check and be certain.

We would recommend visiting a shop that sells greenhouses and walking into a few different sizes. It will help you to visualize the space better and work out which one is best for you. Just remember to avoid the salesperson's charm, or you may end up with a very expensive greenhouse!

When looking for a greenhouse, you need to consider how easy it is for you to maintain and use the greenhouse. If your greenhouse takes a lot of time to maintain each year, then it means less time doing other jobs.

Positioning Your Greenhouse

Where you will put your greenhouse can influence the size, as well as other factors. Obviously, you need to position it, so it gets good sun throughout the day.

Avoid the north-facing slopes as the amount of light will not be sufficient. Do not build your greenhouse at the bottom of a slope, as it is likely to be the location of a frost pocket, meaning cold air will gather around your greenhouse. This makes your greenhouse colder, requiring more heating and reducing the benefits you get from your greenhouse. If you have no choice but to site your greenhouse facing north, which is still better than not having a greenhouse at all!

Depending on your preference, you may choose to align your greenhouse in one of two ways.

Firstly, you can align it, so the sun tracks down one side of the greenhouse. The advantage of this is that one side gets lots of sunlight and the other gets less, allowing you to grow plants that require less sun or need a bit of shade on the side of the greenhouse furthest from the sun.

Alternatively, you can align your greenhouse, so the sun shines on one of the small ends, so the whole greenhouse gets sun throughout the day.

Which you choose is up to you, and it may be that the locations available to you in your vegetable plot influence the alignment.

As an 8x6-inch greenhouse is virtually square, the alignment to the sun is not so important. It becomes more important for larger greenhouses to ensure you maximize the sun for your plants.

Something else to consider is the direction of the prevailing wind in your area. Typically, you will position the door away from the wind. This helps secure your greenhouse and makes it a little less susceptible to wind damage.

You want to position your greenhouse where it is not under trees. Should the trees lose branches, then it will damage or even destroy your greenhouse.

Ideally, you want your greenhouse located in a sheltered spot where it is not going to be subjected to high winds. It may not always be possible, but if you can do this, then it will help prevent damage in the future.

If you are planning on using an irrigation system or installing electricity, then your choice of the site needs to take this into consideration. It needs to be somewhere you can supply these services without too much work or expense. If not, then you are stuck watering by hand and using paraffin or solar heaters like most gardeners!

Choosing the Best Floor

All of these decisions need to be made before you buy your greenhouse, which is probably one of the most controversial!

Which floor you choose will depend a lot on what you are planning on growing in your greenhouse and your environment.

Your choices are:

• No floor, just use the soil.
• The concrete path down the middle, soil to either side.
• The concrete path down the middle, weed membrane on either side.
• Complete concrete floor.

They all have their pros and cons, but it is a personal decision based on your site, budget, and available resources.

The problem with this is that the weed membrane does not extend outside of the greenhouse, meaning the hard-to-reach edges become infested with weeds. This is okay on the left-hand side, but the right-hand side has been staged in place, so it is extremely hard to weed.

The lesson has been learned, and on my next greenhouse, the inside will be much more weed-proof! But back to choosing the best floor for your greenhouse.

The first option is by far the easiest because you don't need to do anything.

The downside of this is the weeds will love the heat in the greenhouse and will thrive. You will have a lot of weeding to do, and this can be very awkward to do when the plants are fully grown.

Some people do grow directly into the soil using bottomless pots. Just be aware that although this option is cheap, you will be battling weeds inside your greenhouse as well as outside.

You also run the risk of introducing soil-borne pests and diseases if you do not change the topsoil in your greenhouse every year or 2.

Having a paved path down the middle of your greenhouse is great as it helps with access and isn't too expensive. You can leave the soil bare on either side or cover it with a weed membrane.

This method works well, as when you put staging in your greenhouse, it becomes very hard to weed underneath it.

Putting weed membrane down will be effective in keeping the weeds away, providing you use a decent quality membrane. Expect to replace it every 2 to 5 years, depending on what you use, as it will perish and eventually allow weeds through.

The final option is by far the best but is also the most expensive as you have to buy paving slabs for the whole greenhouse or poured concrete.

With a larger greenhouse, this can soon become expensive. It is also more work as you have to lay sand and hardcore as well as level the paving.

The advantage of this is that it is a low-maintenance solution. You should get years of a weed-free greenhouse when done properly with a weed membrane under the sand.

As everything will be in pots, you can also move your plants around so you can reposition them as necessary to get them more or less sun as required.

Glass vs. Polycarbonate Panes

Again, this is a personal preference, and both types of panels have their good and bad points. Glass is the more expensive solution, and the most fragile, panels can get broken by accident or vandals and need replacing.

However, glass technology is quite advanced, and you can get some great thermally insulated glass which is ideal for colder areas or heated greenhouses.

Most greenhouses use horticultural glass, which typically comes in 2-inch square panels, so you can end up with overlapping panels. The disadvantage of this type of glass is that it breaks easily into very jagged and sharp pieces. Because of the size, the panels come in, you overlap them, and over time this can become dirty and grow algae, which looks unsightly.

You can buy specially toughened glass for your greenhouse, meaning it isn't going to shatter from a simple touch. It is still breakable, but it will survive an impact from a football though a more solid ball will break it. Just be careful of the edges of toughened glass as that is its weak point. When handling this, make sure you never let the edges touch a rough surface.

Plastic or polycarbonate panels are much cheaper to buy and, for most applications, just as good as glass. The big advantage is that they are a lot harder break which is important if you have kids as accidents do happen.

Because the polycarbonate panels are much lighter than glass, they are also more susceptible to wind damage. In high winds, they can flex and pop out of the frame! Glass is much heavier and gives your greenhouse a more rigid structure, something that is lacking with polycarbonate panels.

Many polycarbonate panels are slightly opaque, meaning you cannot see in or out clearly. It may not bother you, but some people don't like it, and it can reduce the amount of sunlight your plants get.

You should also be aware that most polycarbonate panels are twin-walled, meaning there are two sheets of plastic with an air gap in the middle. Over time water seeps into this gap, and algae forms, which you cannot remove. It has an impact on how much light gets into your greenhouse and also looks untidy. Surprisingly, polycarbonate can cost even more than toughened glass!

Both are easy to get your hands on, being available in many glaziers. Our personal preference is the plastic panels purely from the point of view that they are harder to break and less likely to smash if people throw stones at them.

BEST VEGETABLES TO GROW IN A GREENHOUSE

A greenhouse is excellent for starting your seeds indoors before it's safe to plant seedlings outside. And this will enable you to jump start on the growing season. Nevertheless, you need to harden off the plants so that the change in temperature does not kill them. Those plants that spend the longest time to reach harvest are the best to grow in a greenhouse. For instance, tomatoes work better than do radishes and lettuces. Both radishes and lettuces are short period crops, you can plant all three though. Tomato is better since it takes much longer to turn out a harvest. The following are considered some of the best vegetables to grow in a greenhouse:

- Tomatoes
- Artichoke
- Peas
- Cauliflower
- Kale
- Broccoli
- Arugula
- Collard Greens

Some crops work better in a cold frame instead of a greenhouse, and those include:

- Herbs that love cool weather
- Carrots which don't transplant well
- Salad greens such as lettuces

If you plan to grow the whole crops in the greenhouse, then these plants are the best. Plants such as corn that are wind pollinated may not yield well. If you intend to grow your entire plant in the greenhouse, make sure you take the challenges of pollinating into consideration when choosing the structure's design.

Successive Planting

A perfect tool for successive growing is greenhouse. This equipment can be used to start seeds four to eight weeks before planting. For example, in my area, I sow tomatoes in the middle of March so that they become healthy seedlings and a foot tall or so. Then take them from the seed tray where they germinate to 4-inch containers.

I start heirloom tomatoes seeds 8 weeks earlier than the expected planting date, and I transfer them to one-gallon pots before transplanting them into the ground in mid-May or early June.

When successive gardening is applied, you will foresee the date of harvest for plants and then get ready for your next plant while the current plants are still growing and budding. The essence of this is to make the most use of the smaller growing space of a container to begin your next plant. It means you're raising two gardens at once, but since the following sets of plants are small, they need less space. Going by this, you will gain about six to eight-week decrease in time between one harvest and the next. Therefore, a greenhouse is a tool that helps you boost the overall yield or produce all through your growing season. Almost all plants you will be growing in your garden are the "best" plants to be grown in greenhouses If successive gardening is what you intend. The exceptions are only those plants such as carrots that don't transplant well.

Greenhouse Gardening in Cold Climates

In most parts of the world and the United States, the growing season is shorter or winter is freezing. For these two circumstances, greenhouses are the perfect growing instrument. As I've said earlier, not all plants that thrive in a greenhouse in all season of the year. Some plants require direct sunlight than the others, but using glow light can make up for the lighting needs. Grow the aquarium manufacturing company first used lights to grow plants and corals or home aquariums. Due to the changes to the legal marijuana stand, grow lights are now available at more affordable prices almost everywhere. This implies that you can make up for the drop in direct sunlight by using the artificial lamp for locations with a short growing season.

Shorter days and less night also affect the colder growing weather. For most plants, the decrease in light causes setbacks, but the temperature is another factor. These are the reasons why a greenhouse becomes an instrument to make up for a decrease in warmth and a reduction in lighting.

In both scenarios, those plants that require a warmer growing climate and additional lighting are the best plants to grow in a greenhouse. They can range from vegetables that you intend to grow all year-round, to citrus trees in pots. For year-round growing, it is ideal to opt for plants that grow well in reduced light in the months of winter and where the plants would not be transplanted outside. Some of the plants are:

- Roots such as potatoes, carrots, and other cold-loving plants
- Brassicas such as Cauliflower, broccoli, and Kale
- Herbs
- Lettuces and other greens
- Garlic
- Onions
- Peas

Another method to make up for the cooler temperature in late fall, winter and early spring is to make the most use of a heating technique with your greenhouses. It will allow you to grow crops (such as basil) that are sensitive to a decrease in temperature.

Gardeners use a different type of heating sources to keep their greenhouses warm. The natural way to keep your greenhouse warm is solar radiation. But when the sunlight goes down, the warmth in the greenhouse follow suit. A line of plastic jugs filled with water inside the structure may be all it requires to heat your greenhouse during the night.

Consider installing a heating device if you desire to have more control over the interior temperature of your greenhouse. Both gas and electric heaters are examples of systems that enable you to control the fluctuations of the structure's temperature. You can also use heat lighting methods but may be costly, and anything electric will go down when there is power outage except you have a generator.

Several DIY heating project types are beneficial. Old cast iron wood stoves are easy to install. Inverted flower pot radiator heaters are also great and easy to build. This implies that there are many available options when it comes to heating your greenhouse, which allows you to make the most use of the benefits of greenhouses in different unfavorable climates.

GREENHOUSE PARAMETERS

Location

The location of your greenhouse also depends on many factors. The first factor is the type of plant you want to grow inside your greenhouse.
Tropical plants need maximum sunlight exposure, so you must choose a greenhouse where sunlight comes in an appropriate amount. Most houseplants and flowers need good exposure to sunlight but not direct.
Your location also depends on the climate of your area. If you live in a warm place, then you must need proper shading for your greenhouse.
However, if you live in a cold area, you need maximum sunlight exposure. Remember that the sun changes its position in different seasons.
A very sunny spot in June should not get any sun exposure during the January season, and you must consider this fact before choosing your greenhouse location.

Floor

You have a choice of what kind of floor or base you want for your greenhouse. Many people don't bother to cover their greenhouse base, and they generally have mud or another floor where they constructed their greenhouse. This gives a natural look to your greenhouse. But it is not advisable to keep your floor open because many insects, worms, and rodents may grow inside the mud and should harm your plants. Some base constructions are available with the greenhouse construction kit, and you don't need to buy extra material for your base. But if it is not available in your kit, you can buy it from the market. Concrete floors are a good option for your greenhouse's base as they make the best place to put your benches and other materials. Sometimes, wooden floors are also good for your greenhouse

Foundation

When you are building a greenhouse, the first step is to build a foundation. This needs to be done properly for you to have a solid greenhouse that will stand the test of time. Whatever you decide to make your foundation out of, it needs to be both level and square. It needs to be big enough for the outside dimensions of the greenhouse to ensure it fits properly and can be secured. You can buy pre-made greenhouse bases, and these are worth considering, but just be aware that these still need a flat and level surface to be installed on and will still need a foundation beneath them.

When building your greenhouse base, you can either make it out of poured concrete or use sand and paving stones. Both are suitable and do the job well, though the latter has the advantage of being moveable in the future if necessary.

Ensure that not only are the edges of your base square but also that the diagonal measurements between the corners are also identical.

Under the base, you will need the foundation which is what supports the weight of the greenhouse, which is secured to and prevents damage in windy weather.

If you live in an area where the ground freezes, then your greenhouse foundation needs to be below the frost line. This is to prevent damage to your structure from the ground heaving as it freezes and melts. Your local Building Permit Agency will be able to tell you where the frost line is in your area. In warmer areas, this is only going to be a couple of inches at most, but in the colder, northern areas, it can be as much as a few feet.

One good way of insulating your foundation and protecting it is to use 1-inch foam insulation. Put this down to your frost line to reduce heat loss through the soil, which has the benefit of reducing your heating costs.

The foundation is essential because this is what you are securing your greenhouse too. It will prevent weather damage and warping in hot or cold weather. If you do not secure your greenhouse properly, then don't expect it to last the growing season. If the greenhouse starts to warp, then you can find your panes shatter or crack and become very hard to re-fit. You can also find doors and windows become stiff and very difficult to use too.

If you have bought a new greenhouse, then any warranty will not cover damage due to not having a proper greenhouse base.

Your greenhouse is built on this foundation and base, which will ensure it is easier to erect and that it will last. There are some different choices for the foundation, which we'll talk about now.

Compacted Soil

If you compact the soil enough, then you can build your greenhouse directly on the ground, particularly if you live in an area where the ground doesn't freeze too badly.

A lot of greenhouses will come with an optional metal plinth that has spiked in each corner. These can be cemented into the ground to prevent the base from moving.

You will still need to level the ground, though, so dig out your spirit level. Use a roller or other mechanical device to compact the soil to ensure it is stable. Do not build your base out of gravel or hardcore because these are just not stable enough.

The advantage of using the soil as your foundation is that it is very cost-effective. You can also use the existing ground to grow your plants, plus drainage is a lot better.

The downside of soil is that it will allow pests into your greenhouse. You will find this particularly bad in winter as pests flock to your greenhouse for the warmth.

Perimeter Bases

This is a slightly cheaper option where you use either bricks, breeze blocks, or thin paving or edging slabs to create a foundation directly under the greenhouse frame. You can use concrete if you prefer.

The foundation is built along where the frame will run, leaving the soil untouched in the middle of the greenhouse.

While you can build the foundation directly on the soil, most people will cut out a trench and place the foundation in the trench. The advantage of this latter approach is that it is easier to level.

Slabs or Paving

This is a very popular way to build your greenhouse foundation because it keeps out the weeds and pests while giving you a good, clean, growing environment.

This method involves building a base the size of your greenhouse out of paving slabs and then fixing your greenhouse to it. This type of base will last for many years and is very low maintenance.

You can screw your greenhouse to the base to provide stability in windy conditions, preventing any damage. It also provides good drainage when compared to an all-concrete base.

In the winter months, a soil floor can get damp and encourage mold to grow. A paved floor helps to keep the greenhouse both warmer and drier in the cooler months.

Providing you bed down the slabs properly with an inch or two of sand underneath them, they are surprisingly easy to get level and will not warp or move over time.

Concrete Base

This is where you mark out where your greenhouse will be and dig down a few inches before pouring concrete in to form the base.

For larger greenhouses, this has its advantages, but it can be expensive and does require special tools such as a concrete mixer.

This is a very durable base, and you can fit expansion bolts to secure larger structures. You may have an issue with standing water, so you may want to consider putting drainage holes in to prevent standing water.

Plastic Resin

These are very attractive and are very popular. This is because, compared to aluminum, they are less expensive, and they also do not conduct any heat away from the greenhouse-like steel does.

Unfortunately, they lack the strength of the metal frames, and can only be used for the smaller greenhouses, with shorter dimensions.
They can only be used with polycarbonate panels.

Wood

Wooden frames are ideal for a simple do-it-yourself greenhouse project. Wood is beautiful and provides sufficient durability and strength, but it is susceptible to rotting; therefore, it doesn't allow contact with moisture.

Tempered Glass

These are strong and impact-resistant.
This means that they will withstand any expansions or contractions during the seasonal temperature changes.
The 3 mm single pane thickness is ideal for the greenhouse.
However, the 4mm thickness is much stronger and will provide additional insulation.
You must protect the hedges during insulation, as the glass may shatter if hit hard.
Tempered glass is much more expensive compared to polycarbonate panels.
Tempered glass is more durable even if it's expensive, and it is more resistant to scratches and is very clear and provides no diffusion.

Fiberglass

This is translucent and provides a light that is well-diffused. Fiberglass retains heat better than normal glass. The greenhouses made from fiberglass are normally corrugated to provide adequate rigidity because the outer coat will become sunbaked within 6-10 years. The surface will become etched and yellow.

Polycarbonate

It is UV-treated, lightweight and durable. It is high quality and modern material used for greenhouses. The polycarbonate is available in different levels of thickness and provides the clarity of glass, but it's not scratch resistant, or as strong as tempered glass.
The single-walled one does not retain any heat and provides no light diffusion. It, however, has a longer lifespan of more than 15 years, depending on the region.

Twin-Walled Polycarbonate

This is very popular because it has internal spaces providing strength and excellent insulation. The best point to note about the twin-walled polycarbonate is that it diffuses light.

Triple-Walled Polycarbonate

This is similar to twin-walled polycarbonate, but it has extra strength and heat retention abilities. In cold climates, the triple-walled polycarbonate is extremely useful for all-year-round indoor gardening, because it will withstand snow loads and will freeze without cracking or distorting.

Wind Securities

Any surface such as a wall, fence, or even nearby buildings can act as protection against gusts of wind or even snow. When plants are close to these surfaces, they can leech onto the small amount of warmth that they provide. If your plants cannot stand the heat during summer, you can use these surfaces as sunblock.

BEST GREENHOUSE EQUIPMENT AND ACCESSORIES

Efficient greenhouse equipment and accessories can be critical to the successful operation of the greenhouse.

To be able to grow high-quality, year-round crops, you would need to know what kind of greenhouse equipment you need to buy. Let's look at the best greenhouse equipment and supplies required when beginning greenhouse gardening:

One of the main features of an effective greenhouse design is getting the right accessories to make growing crops easier:

1. Basic
2. Greenhouse Furniture
3. Water Management — Irrigation and Drainage
4. Lighting
5. Heating and Climate control
6. Ventilation
7. Pest Control

Each of these components must be prepared for the design of the greenhouses. As you read on, we're going to explore the various things that come in each group.

These are the fundamental things that you need to start growing plants.

Container

Your choice of greenhouse containers is essential because it will significantly influence how your vegetables or plants grow. Gardeners can use almost anything that grips the soil as long as it meets two criteria for a greenhouse container:

• First, it should promote good health, provide plenty of rooting space and provide excellent drainage.

• Second, it should keep the crop well and stabilize its upward production.

There are different kinds of containers, such as flats and tubes, hanging baskets, and pans.

There are also larger containers that are designed to accommodate a variety of smaller pots.

Hanging baskets are ideal for growing plants, flowers, and vegetables in height while making good use of space. It can be made of plastic, metal-ceramic, or even coconut fiber.

Plugs and flat containers are also used for early germination purposes. These containers are available to accommodate several small plants or flowers while keeping them apart. As far as potting is concerned, gardeners prefer greenhouse pots made of clay because they are the traditional way to grow flowers and plants. However, you can also consider plastic, wood, peat moss, and wood fiber materials. They are also lighter in weight, more durable, and cheaper than clay pots. They're also easily disposable.

Seed Boxes

Seed boxes are also considered essential greenhouse equipment. Plastic seed boxes take over from the wooden boxes used by many growers in the past. The pros and cons of plastic against wood are still being explored across the world. If you want to go green, cut off the plastic option and stick with the wood. However, get seed boxes that are around 14 inches X 8 inches X 2 inches. It is the ideal size for rising baby seeds. Rain Chains like these copper rain chains are another perfect product touch.

Furniture to Store Your Greenhouse Equipment and Plants

Well-planned furniture plus adequate shelving inside a greenhouse is essential for the storage of all your pots and containers. Shelving in a tight, space-limited greenhouse system will improve the growing area without negative impacts on the shade.
Shelves may be made from materials such as glass, wood, or metal. It is necessary to note that the amount of lighting entering plants can be affected if double shelving is used. You can also find shelves under garden benches to save space. Greenhouse shelves may be temporary for starting seedlings or permanently attached to the greenhouse structure. Cinder, wooden blocks, and metal are suitable for legs and tables. The wire mesh of the shelves makes it possible to remove excess water. Greenhouse shelving can also help keep crops apart to avoid seeding or cross-pollination. Garden benches are one type of shelving that allows maximum room and storage.
In general, their ideal size is determined by the width of the hothouse to maximize the through space. Benches can be permanent or temporary fixtures. If you plan to delete or rearrange them regularly, sectioned bench options can be ideal.
Planters are another kind of greenhouse furniture that is commonly used in today's gardening environment. Large and deep seedlings are generally recommended for food crops. They can be made from a range of materials, such as plastic, wood, or metal. They are usually organized in such a way that each planter contains only one vegetable.

Greenhouse Irrigation and Drainage

Systems over their lifetimes, you will need ways to water your plants. Though automatic watering systems are all crazy, there will always be a special place for good old watering cans in traditional gardening. T
he long beams on the cans will comfortably touch all the plants, including at the back of the flower bed.

Greenhouse Water Management

Likewise, you will be able to customize your watering experience depending on what each bed needs. Plastics also take over metal in the watering can section. Plastic containers are usually smaller, making watering less labor-intensive. Plus, they're also cheaper. But if you have greenhouse aesthetics, stick to the metal cans. The trickle watering system is another form of greenhouse equipment.

Greenhouse Trickle Watering System

Build a plastic hose rinse system with outlet nozzles at various intervals across its duration. Place the hose around your pots in acceptable proximity. Attach your hose to a storage tank that keeps filling and releases water when it's finished. What's great about this system is that you're going to water your pots or beds in the exact quantity you want, at the exact time every day!
Other types of greenhouse water treatment equipment that you may need are good pumps, water breakers, valves, pumps, hoses, sprinklers, and temperature control boilers. Remember, you're going to have to find a place in your greenhouse or yard to store these things.

Greenhouse Lighting

The lighting system inside the greenhouse determines the level of sunlight, artificial light, and shade of the plants. If the sunlight in your area isn't strong enough, you might need to consider artificial lighting.
• Grow lights
• Seedling lights
• Leds
• General all-purpose lighting
• High-intensity lights
Providing a vast lighting network can be costly for small greenhouses, for larger ones, it is almost necessary.

Climate Control and Heating Greenhouse Equipment

These are often a few types of greenhouse equipment designed to control the amount of moisture, heat, and frost inside the greenhouse. Let's look at the main components of the climate control system:

Greenhouse Thermometers

The key to a successful greenhouse is to maintain perfect temperatures at all times, making the thermometer very important. Install a maximum and minimum temperature thermometer with a needle location that appears when the mercury is removed. When it comes to greenhouse thermometers, you're going to need one that can be reset with a magnet.
There are more high-end options with push-button readjustments, but they are not necessary. All types of greenhouses, even portable ones, require thermometers. Often, call a soil thermometer to determine the temperature of the soil.

Greenhouse Thermostat

A greenhouse thermostat helps you know the current temperature in your greenhouse and control it accordingly. The temperature gauge or thermometer indicates the temperature changes while the thermostat automatically controls the temperature in the desired area. Ideally, a good greenhouse is expected to have a thermostat.

Greenhouse Heaters

Other critical greenhouse equipment deals with the control of heat inside the greenhouse. Greenhouse heaters are needed to control the temperature of the greenhouse. They come in different types, with different modes and sources of energy. You can choose from electric, gas, and propane heaters according to your needs and requirements. You also have the choice of either choosing a sold or non-vented heater.

Greenhouse Humidistat

Greenhouse humidifiers or humidistats are needed to check the quantity of moisture in the greenhouse. Some plants are sensitive to dry air, which will impede their vegetative growth. With the aid of an appropriate humidistat, this problem can easily be solved.

Ventilation Equipment for Your Greenhouse

Proper ventilation is compulsory for adequate plant growth, not only during certain seasons but throughout the year. This is because, at any time of year, the sun is capable of causing extreme temperature changes. A reasonable rule of thumb is to have open venting options equal to around 20% of the floor space. Vents can be found on the roof and sides of the structure as well as part of the entrance. Roof venting is considered to be the absolute best when it comes to fixing venting systems. Many automated venting systems are the perfect choices for those who are not around to handle the greenhouse all day. Exhaust fans are another way to vent excess air, but whether or not they are a good option for any case, in particular, they deserve analysis.

Pest Control Equipment

No list of greenhouse equipment will be full without pest control equipment. There are several methodologies for effective pest control; some use chemicals, and others use biology. Chemicals are easy to use and relatively cheap, but others may argue that they do more harm than good.

Natural methods, such as the use of what is generally referred to as "beneficial insects," are another type of pest control. Mostly, these bugs track down and eat the bugs that kill your garden. Often all the plant wants is a decent mesh to keep the pests out. These meshes may be made of metal, fabric, or thin plastic. You would also need fencing and door sweeps to keep bugs out of particular areas. Various kinds of fogging machines and sprayers kill bugs. Insecticides and pesticides should be used sparingly, ideally using organic or natural sprays to prevent pests from damaging crops.

Soil Sterilizers

Whatever soil you are considering for planting, it would be extremely helpful to make use of a sterilizer. There are several ways to sterilize the soil, but the easiest and most effective way to do so is by using a steam sterilization system. Steam systems are advantageous and inexpensive. They're not going to take up a lot of space and do a fantastic job on your soil.

Gardening Sieve – Sowing Sieve

The soil texture is an important consideration when planting baby plants. A sowing sieve will be very useful in helping you to achieve the perfect texture. You can use a mesh sieve to cover your seeds with compost after you plant them gently. The good news is that you don't necessarily need to buy a sieve. This piece of greenhouse equipment could be a DIY idea.

Use a small wooden box like those in which you buy bulk produce. Take the bottom of the box and put a piece of perforated zinc in it, and voila — you've got your sieve! You can also assign this essential task to your children and your relatives.

Plant Support Equipment

You will need to provide adequate support to ensure that your plants grow in strength and length. Sometimes, all you have to do is tie the plants together so that they can support each other. Although there are many materials used to bind your plants, we recommend Raphia as it is moderately priced and can help most plants. Many greenhouse growers often use broken loops, green growing twines, and paper-covered wires. Fencing and greenhouse molds can also be used to shape plants into the desired shapes.

GROWING HERBS IN A GREENHOUSE

Using a greenhouse to grow herbs like other plants, allow you to control the heat, moisture, and shade for your plants, giving them a perfect environment in which to grow.

Herbs growing in a greenhouse will shelter tender annual crops from the excessive summer heat. It also extends the season and provides an enabling environment for your plants to thrive earlier and later in the season. Setting up your greenhouse before adding a single plant is crucial to getting the most out of it.

Set up automatic drip hoses and a misting system to guarantee a stable supply of moisture to your plants. Insufficient humidity is one of the most common reasons herbs fail. Installing automatic systems that offer a regular, slowly amount of water daily will ensure steady growth of herbs.

System of shading plants is another crucial factor for growing herbs in greenhouses. If you are constructing a new greenhouse, do not create a roof made wholly of glass. Some sunroof or skylights type installations are suitable for aeration, but some herbs require shading from the brightest of the daylight sun. If you have already constructed your greenhouse, create a shading system using rip-stop nylon and Velcro or hooks to attach to the roof. This system can be easily connected and removed depending on the plant's needs.

Types of Herbs for Greenhouses

The best herbs you can grow in greenhouses are those tender annuals which are very sensitive to the average traditional garden or any herb you desire to grow in a more extended season than usual. The following are some of the common herbs you can grow in greenhouses:

- Basil
- Cilantro
- Chives
- Chamomile
- Dill
- Mints
- Parsley

How to Grow Basil in a Greenhouse

Basil can be grown as much indoors much the same as you it could in the garden. You can grow the magnificent, scent basil for making aromatic oils, kitchen use, and for aesthetic purposes.

Basil growing in a greenhouse is easy. Plant it in a well-drained container inside your greenhouse, and nutrient-rich soil. It's imperative to use the top quality soil to be successful in growing basil in a container. This herb cannot tolerate water stress; ensure the containers have sufficient drainage. The soil must be kept slightly moist though, but never should it becomes soggy if not, the roots would be subjected to rotting.

Basil growing in a greenhouse will need to be fertilized, depending on the type you are growing and the purpose of growing it. You can use a general houseplants fertilizer. However, if you are growing it for flavoring foods, make use of organic fertilizer. Using organic fertilizer will also help to keep pH levels when growing basil in a greenhouse. Healthy levels of pH are another crucial factor of good soil. You will be sure to check the soil pH levels every 4-6 weeks or once in a month for the best possible growth. Adequate soil pH levels usually are between 6.0 and 7.5.

Besides, lighting is vital factor when growing basil in a greenhouse, the plant needs nothing less than 6 hours of sunlight. Basil should be positioned in a sunny area, if possible facing south. If not, you may need to place the plants under fluorescent lights. If grown under fluorescent light, basil will require about ten hours of light for it to grow well. Nevertheless, you can supply basil grown in a greenhouse with both sunlight and artificial lighting by alternating them.

How to Grow Cilantro in greenhouse

Cilantro growing in a greenhouse can be flavorful as growing it in a traditional garden when given a little more care. It's ideal to start growing cilantro with starter plants or seed as it doesn't transplant well. Also, ensure that your plants are three to four inches apart.

The best container for growing cilantro is unglazed terra cotta for the reason that it gives room for better moisture and air to pass through the roots. Ensure there are sufficient drainage holes in the base of the pot. Cilantro growing in a greenhouse requires more nourishment as it has limited root system range and cannot access as much of soil nutrients as it will in a traditional garden. When planting in a greenhouse, mix the potting soil with sand to enable water to move freely. Additionally, you can use liquid fish emulsion fertilizer to provide extra nutrients. During the active growing season, use half concentration of the fertilizers bi-weekly. When growing cilantro in a greenhouse, it requires more thorough watering than frequent watering. Keep watering the plants until water begins to come out of the drainage holes. However, cilantro must only be watered when the soil is dry to touch, so check the soil regularly as the dryness would be more often in summer periods. Another vital factor when growing cilantro in a greenhouse is that the plants must receive 4-5 hours full sun per day.

Harvesting Cilantro

When harvesting cilantro in a greenhouse, handling it carefully is essential. Indoor herbs reach for the light and may become spindly as a result. Pinch them at the growing tips to force a bushier plant. Remember that cilantro grown indoors will not grow as abundantly as when grown in the traditional garden. Nevertheless, with extra care and attention to soil mixture, moisture, sun exposure, and careful harvesting, you would be rewarded with this aromatic and flavorful herb year round.

How to Grow Parsley in greenhouses

Parsley will grow well in a sunny area, especially when facing south where they would receive 6-8 hours of direct sun daily. Supplement with fluorescent light if your greenhouse does not receive that much sunlight. Rotate the container every 3-4 days so that the plants don't lean to the sun.

Grow parsley in pots the same way you grow other potted herbs. Use a container with many drainage holes and a saucer beneath to hold water as it drains. Use top-quality potting soil and add a reasonable amount of sand to improve the drainage. You will need to mist the plants periodically. If the leaves seem brittle and dry, place the plant on a tray of gravel and add water to the tray, exposing the tops of the gravel. It will increase the air's humidity around the plant as the water evaporates.

Begin growing parsley by sowing seeds directly in the pot because it has a long tap root that is not good for transplanting. Spread a few seeds on the soil's surface and cover them with another 1/4 inch of soil. Water the container frequently for soil to remain moderately moist but not soggy, and be expecting the seedling to germinate within three weeks. If the emerged seedlings are too many, you will have to thin them out. Pinch the excess out between your thumb and fingernail or clip them out with scissors. Pulling them out can harm the tap roots of the nearby plants.

Caring for parsley in greenhouse

Greenhouse parsley care is simple. Keep the soil relatively humid, and drain the saucer underneath the container after every watering to prevent the roots from sitting in water. Feed the plants every two weeks with half-strength liquid fertilizer or fish emulsion.

If you wish, you can grow parsley with other herbs in the container. Examples of herbs that go well with parsley in a mixed container are basil, chives, mint, oregano, and thyme. When growing thyme with parsley, plant them around the edges of the pot where they can stumble over the sides.

TEMPERATURE AND HUMIDITY FOR A GREENHOUSE

Airflow is very important for healthy plant growth in a greenhouse, particularly in the heat of summer as temperatures (hopefully) soar. The air needs to keep moving which will prevent heat from building up and damaging your plants.

Most greenhouses will come with vents and/or windows to help with the movement of air. A good quality greenhouse will have louver vents at ground level that draw in cold air (which is heavier than hot air) and then vents at the top, allowing hot air to rise out of the greenhouse. This creates a very natural movement of air which your plants appreciate.

You are looking for a greenhouse with windows and vents that account for around a third of the entire roof area. They do not all need to be at roof level and, ideally, you will want vents at different levels.

If your greenhouse isn't suitably ventilated, you will encourage all sorts of diseases such as fungal problems, powdery mildew, and botrytis. Worse still a greenhouse that is too hot will end up killing some of your plants.

You can leave the door open in the summer, but this can be a security problem depending on where your greenhouse is located.

The other disadvantage of leaving a door open is that pets, particularly cats, will decide to investigate your greenhouse. Dogs, cats, and chickens will cause havoc in your greenhouse from eating plants and fruits to sitting on plants. If you do have pets and want to leave the door open, then a wire panel will keep out most animals except cats. Window or door screens can be used to keep out unwanted visitors, but the downside of these is that they can also keep out vital pollinating insects!

Mice and other rodents can find their way into your greenhouse through open windows or doors so it can be worth installing an ultrasonic device to keep them out. Of course, cats are excellent rodent deterrents but cause their unique brand of chaos!

Shade Cloth and Paint

This is one of the simplest ways for you to provide shade for your plants.

Shade paint is applied to the outside of your glass, and it diffuses the sun and keeps some of the heat out. Modern shade paints are very clever and will react to the sunlight. When it is raining then the shade paint remains clear, but as the sun comes out, the paint turns white, reflects the sunlight.

Shade fabric is another way to cool your greenhouse, and this is put on the outside of your greenhouse to prevent the sunlight from getting to your plants. It is best installed on the outside of your greenhouse, but you can put it inside, though it will not be as effective. When it is outside, it stops the sun's rays from penetrating your greenhouse but when on the inside the sunlight is already in the greenhouse and generating heat.

Shading alone though is not going to protect your plants from heat damage. Combine this with good ventilation and humidity control to provide your plants with the best possible growing environment.

Shade cloth is a lightweight polyethylene knitted fabric available in densities from 30% to 90% to keep out less or more of the sun's rays. It is not only suitable for greenhouses but is used in cold frames and other applications. It is mildew and rot resistant, water permeable, and does not become brittle over time.

It provides great ventilation and diffuses the light, keeping your greenhouse cooler. It can help reduce the need to run fans in the summer and install and remove quickly.

A reflective shade is good because instead of absorbing the sun's rays it reflects them. This is better if you can get hold of it because it will be more efficient at keeping the greenhouse cool. The reflective shade cloth is more expensive than a normal shade cloth, but it is worth the money for the additional benefits.

For most applications, you will want a shade cloth that is 50–60% density, but in hotter climates or with light-sensitive plants higher densities such as 70–80% will be necessary. A lot of people use higher-density shade cloth on the roof and lower-density cloth on the walls.

Shade cloth is typically sold by the foot or meter, depending on where you are located, though you can find it sold in pre-made sizes. These are usually hemmed and include grommets for attaching the cloth to the greenhouse.

Shade cloth with a density of 70% allows 30% of light to pass through it. For most vegetables, in the majority of climates, a shade cloth of 30–50% will be sufficient. If you are shading people, then you will want to go up to a density of 80–90%.

Air Flow

During summer, keeping the air moving in your greenhouse can be difficult, particularly in larger greenhouses. Many of the larger electrical greenhouse heaters will double up as air blowers in the summer just by using the fan without the heating element been turned on.

However, using a fan is down to whether or not you have electricity in your greenhouse, which not all of us will have. Although you can use solar energy to run your fan, you will find that it is hard to generate enough energy to keep it going all day.

Automatic Vents

These are an absolute godsend for any gardener and will help keep your plants alive and stop you from having to get up early to open vents!

Automatic vents will open the windows as the temperature rises. This is usually by a cylinder of wax which expands in the heat, opening the window, and then contracts as the temperature cools which closes the window. These do have a finite lifetime, typically lasting a few years but are easily replaced.

One technique that can help keep your greenhouse cool is to damp down the paths and the floor. As the water evaporates, it will help keep the greenhouse cool.

Choosing an Exhaust Fan

For larger greenhouses, you will want an exhaust fan. This is overkill for a smaller greenhouse, but anyone choosing a larger structure will benefit from installing one. Your exhaust fan needs to be able to change the air in your greenhouse in between 60 and 90 seconds. Fans are rated by cubic feet per minute (CFM), for which you will need to calculate the volume of your greenhouse which is done simply by multiplying the length by the width by the average height.

To measure the average height, measure straight down to the floor from halfway up a roof rafter. It doesn't have to be precise as a few inches either way isn't going to make a significant difference.

To determine the cubic feet per minute rating, you need you simply multiply the volume by ¾. Then you will need to find a fan that is near to or greater than this value.

Be careful and double-check your calculations as a fan that is too small will not provide you with enough cooling. Together with a fan, shading cloth or paint, and damping down it will help ensure the greenhouse is kept cool and your plants thrive.

Although your greenhouse may be too small for a fan or you may not have any electricity, at the very least you need windows though louver vents will help a lot. Making sure there is adequate ventilation in your greenhouse is vital so don't skip this step when setting up your greenhouse!

SEED STARTING

One of the biggest benefits of a greenhouse is it gives you somewhere to start your seedlings off, so you get a head start on the growing season. Even a small, plastic portable greenhouse out in your garden is sufficient to start your seeds off, and the extra warmth means you can get a really good head start on the year.

Germinating seeds is something many of us will do every year, but it is often touch-and-go as to whether or not they will germinate. It can be hard to find enough space to germinate all the seeds that you want to plant, and you end up not planting some crops you wanted to grow. A greenhouse is a real boon because it gives you plenty of space to start your seeds in a protected environment.

You then need a decent growing medium. A good, peat-based seed compost is a good place to start though you can mix up your own formulas. Avoid cheap compost because it tends to dry out very quickly, has large lumps in, and is not as good for your seedlings. You can find your seeds rot before they germinate because the cheap compost doesn't drain well.

Seed trays and containers are good to get, and we often use ones with plastic lids. This way, we can have a greenhouse within a greenhouse.

There are a huge variety of seed trays on the market, depending on what you're growing, use different seed trays. Larger cell trays are used for larger plants, whereas open trays are used for seeds that can be scattered like beetroot, carrot, and so on.

For some seeds, such as sweetcorn, cardboard tubes (such as those found inside toilet rolls) are good to use because the seedlings do not like being handled. The tubes can be planted straight in the ground, and the cardboard will rot as the seedling grows.

Larger plants such as squashes are best sown in individual pots so they can grow to a decent size without having to be re-potted, which they can object to.

You can use peat pots to grow your seedlings in though I have found these have a habit of either drying out too much or becoming sodden and then rotting. Some people like these but I'm not keen on them.

All of these can be sat in seed trays to make it easier for you to organize your plants. Just remember that you have to pick out your seedlings and re-pot them when they get to a certain size and certain types of plants will not appreciate this.

Heat mats can be used to help with germination, but they are not necessary. If you live in a really cold climate, they are a benefit, but it requires that you have electricity in your greenhouse, which not everyone will have. You also have the expense of buying the heat mats, so you may get one or two to start off your most important or delicate seedlings.

You need to think about the light requirements of each plant because some seedlings prefer more light to others. More sun-sensitive seedlings will need shading from the heat of the midday sun.

When sowing seeds in individual pots, one useful technique is to place two or three seeds into each pot, spaced out evenly. This way, if one or two seeds do not germinate, you still have a third which could grow. If all three grow, then you can either prick out and re-plant the three seedlings, or you can discard the smaller seedlings, keeping the strongest.

All seeds need to be covered by the growing medium but not too deeply otherwise, they will not push through the soil to the light. Check the packets to determine exactly how deeply to plant each seed.

For bigger seeds, it is easy to poke them into the soil. One thing to remember with larger seeds, such as squash seeds, is to plant them on their sides so they can grow the right way up. If they are put in the ground the wrong way, then you can find the roots coming up through the soil and the leaves growing underground! This often happens when children help with the planting.

For smaller seeds, you need to cover them with a sprinkling of soil to stop them from blowing away. With smaller seeds, you will need to be careful watering them as they can float away with excess water!

Seeds can take anything from a few days to a few weeks to germinate, depending on the plant you grow. Check the packet for specific timings, so you know when to start checking your seedlings.

During this time, you need to keep them moist, but not wet otherwise, the seeds can rot. Check the pots regularly and make sure they are not too damp. Peat pots can go moldy if the humidity is too high, so you need to keep an eye on them too.

Check the instructions and plant during the time they state. Remember that you can start your seedlings earlier in cooler areas than you can outside with a greenhouse.

Hardening Off

Not all of your seedlings are going to spend their lives in your greenhouse; some will be planted outside. Moving a plant from the protective enclosure that is your greenhouse into the great outdoors can be an incredible shock to the system. The difference in environments causes shock, which can at best stunt your plant's growth by several weeks, and at worst, kill it!

Hardening off your seedlings is vital if you want them to survive and thrive when you plant them outside of your greenhouse. You will be surprised how many people don't do this and struggle to get their plants to grow.

The process of hardening off isn't done overnight and can take a week or two, depending on the weather where you live. You will have to be patient, but it is worth it as it strengthens your plants and ensures they grow well.

Once there is no risk of frost during the day, you take your seedlings out of your greenhouse and leave them outside during the day. Put them somewhere that is warm but not too sunny, and that is sheltered from the wind.

Leave your seedlings outside for most of the day, and then mid to late afternoon, move them back into your greenhouse.

Repeat this for 2 or 3 days and then gradually move them into sunnier locations and leave them out for longer.

After a couple of weeks, the seedlings should be in the location where they are to be planted and be left out all day and throughout the night.

Should your plants show any sign of stress such as browning, wilting, or yellowing, then move the hardening process back a step and try again the following day.

Water well during this process, and then after the 2 weeks, you should be able to plant your seedlings out in the ground. It is worth observing them as some may benefit from horticultural fleece or a cloche if the weather starts to get cold or if there is a surprise frost.

Sorting Your Seed Packets

Most gardeners will have seeds packets pretty much everywhere, in drawers, on shelves, tucked away in cupboards. They accumulate, and it is far too easy to get overwhelmed by them. You know what it is like, you get halfway through the growing season and realize you forgot to plant something because you couldn't find the seeds!
There are plenty of different ways for you to organize your seed packets, and it is up to you how best you do it. However, we would strongly recommend that you do organize them because it will make your life easier throughout the growing season and save you money from buying duplicate seed packets.

Firstly, sort the seeds into three piles:

1. Herbs
2. Flowers
3. Vegetables

These are stored separately. Each seed packet is filed under the first month in which it can be planted. Remember that if a seed packet states it can be planted out in a month, then you can often start the seedling off in a greenhouse between 4 and 8 weeks earlier, depending on whether it is heated or not!
A greenhouse is a real boon when it comes to starting off seedlings and will help you get a head start on the growing season. It also gets the seed trays out of the house and gives your plants a great start in life. Many growers tend to ask the difference between vegetables, herbs, and fruits. A vegetable is a plant or any part of a plant that is considered edible and can be eaten. On the other hand, Herbs refer to plants or parts of plants that are grown as food and also for medicinal purposes while fruits are eatable products containing seeds formed from the matured ovary of a flowering plant. The major difference is that while fruits can be referred to as vegetables, vegetables cannot exactly be termed fruits. Also, it is arguable that not all herbs are eaten as the main ingredient, as is the case of vegetables.

MAINTAINING YOUR GREENHOUSE
To keep a greenhouse, the first thing you need to consider is the cost, depending on several factors. Like I have mentioned before, greenhouses are available in a variety of shapes and sizes. So its maintenance will vary from one garden to another. The information I'm about to discuss will be based on the most economical ways of maintaining your greenhouse to be sure you don't end up emptying your wallet. Another question to ask is how hard is it to maintain a greenhouse? The same is applicable to every hobby; being a beginner can be a determinant of whether you will find something hard or not. But I can assure you that mastering and following the below tips will make it easy for you to maintain your greenhouse.

Maintain a Constant Temperature in Your Greenhouse

Keeping a steady temperature is one of the most crucial factors in ensuring proper maintenance of your greenhouse. To accomplish this, you can:

- Purchase and make use of readily available monitoring systems. The work of some operations is not limited to monitoring the internal temperature of the greenhouse, but also checks the moisture and acidity of your soil, which are also very important.
- Consider using an evaporative cooling system as this is very popular as it cools the air inside with water. It is evident that most plants grow well in a moist and humid environment; this makes it an ideal choice if you want to maintain a constant temperature. Having a proper cooling system is one of the best and affordable ways of maintaining a greenhouse.
- Ventilation is another crucial factor to consider. Given that greenhouses naturally trap heat from sunlight, the temperature may be drastically increased. And this can be avoided by having proper aeration. You might need to consider installing an air conditioning unit if opening windows and doors proved insufficient. Also, installing airflow fans will help improve circulation. Another good idea is having lots of vents in your greenhouse surroundings.
- Lighting is also an essential factor in maintaining a stable temperature inside the greenhouse. It is necessary when you're growing plants that aren't in season. Apart from light, you may also buy heaters. Some heaters are very easy to use as they are automatically regulated.

Maintaining humidity in a greenhouse

Do not apply excessive water on your plants. If you have puddles of water, the moisture tends to increase. Applying water directly to the soil (not to the leaves) will also help to reduce evaporation.

Maintaining a greenhouse in winter

If you don't buy the idea of high-end heating systems, then the following budget-friendly tips will be of help:

Use bubble wraps. You can purchase horticulture bubble wraps at a nursery. Just remember that the larger bubble holds more light than the smaller one. Also, remember to use thermostat. If your heater already has a thermostat, then that's a plus, since the heater can be set only when needed. By always checking, a good thermostat will help, you will be able to know when a heater is needed and when not. Therefore, it will save you money and resources.

Be sure to place your heater in the right spot, where it would work most effectively. As part of the greenhouse maintenance budget rules, it's best to put electric fan heaters in an open area of the structure. Most preferably, place them in the centre. If your greenhouse is larger, heating the entire area may be costly. In this case, you may divide the structure into smaller spaces so you can decide what area to be heated.

Greenhouse Environmental Control Systems

Technology advancement has made owning and running greenhouses simpler than ever before. Options of environmental control help the professional horticulturist or home gardener by automatically adjusting light intensity, humidity, and temperature from a remote location or within the greenhouse. A system of environmental control would enhance plant life within the structure by offering a continually monitored atmosphere, producing a more consistent yield.

You can automate your greenhouse environmental control systems according to your requirements. Greenhouse accessories are pre-set in phases in line with the plant's needs and gardener's choice. These systems present the most significant advantage by providing the facility to control light intensity, adjust humility, adjust the temperature, and monitor the atmosphere, to mention some of the operations.

Accessories Controlled

Cooling systems, heating systems, fogging, systems, misting systems, vents, and fans are all controlled by control systems. The operations could be very straightforward and offer an immense benefit to keeping your greenhouses in ideal shape.

The first phase of execution could be as simple as on/off switch to control fans circulation. By semi-automating a control system using a timing device, a thermostat, or a humidistat, the accessories will run only when necessary; this saves energy and reduces the operating costs. A fully automated system can be controlled through a cell phone, by remote programming system on a PC, or semaphore, saving a considerable amount of time. The fully automated system could be programmed to keep a particular set of condition for stable plant comfort, putting into consideration the circumstances outside the structure which might affect the growth of plants.

Advantages of Automated System

Improve Vegetation Quality: Mimicking a more cold night temperature boosts the quality of vegetation as it more directly simulates the natural environment. Precise humidity and temperature control offer consistent growing conditions to improve production and quality.

Reduce fuel costs: Lowering the temperature of a greenhouse at night when eighty percent of the heating takes place, lessens energy consumption. Centralizing temperature sensors, controlling them with a single unit, prevents cooling and heating systems from running concurrently.

Increase Production: An automated system permits you to focus on growing the plants, not adjusting settings.

Advanced Accessories

Additionally to regular greenhouses accessories, environmental control systems could be programmed to contain advanced elements like remote programming, semaphore, soil sensors, photo and light sensors, drip systems, foggers, and coolers. Your time can now be spent tending to plants instead of messing with their growing environment. Asides the time and cost-effectiveness of the greenhouse control system, Mother Nature will also benefit. Control systems lessen the use of chemicals to aid the growth of plants as the environment is more closely adjusted to produce the perfect condition and reduce energy costs and waste. Here are some of the greenhouses advance accessories:

1. Greenhouse Benches: These benches will make performing gardening functions stress-free. Whether you're transplanting, pruning, potting, or washing farm produce, benches provide space and height utilization alternatives. The greenhouse benches are built to complement any existing or new structure. The polyethylene grid-top and galvanized mesh offer good drainage and air circulation while allowing light to pass through to the plants underneath.

2. Raised Seedling Beds: Seeding beds are another fantastic accessory for greenhouses. Unlike conventional greenhouse benches, they extend growing beyond only pots. A seedling bed is about six inches deep and is supported on four legs. It is often filled with soil for growing plants. Seedling beds are ideal for bringing a vegetable garden or flower bed straight into the greenhouse. With this, you don't have to get on your knees to plant and tend the garden as the bed is raised.

3. Gravel Bench: This is specially used to produce moisture. This type of bench is tailored for use in greenhouses or with plants such as orchids. You can use a fixed bench built with a metal top rather than a conventional mesh top. To apply, fill the top of the bench with gravel and water to create a source of moisture for the flowers.

4. Grow Lights: A greenhouse such as a lean-to with low light and conventional side walls or ceiling wouldn't generate the amount of natural heat needed by specific plants. The addition of grow light is a simple solution. There are also conversion lighting kits. The grow light permits high-pressure sodium light bulb and metal halide to be interchanged. You can rotate the bulbs as the greenhouse advances, and plants selections change. These lightings promote new growth and keep plants healthy. Nowadays, there are several forms of grow light in the market; for example, compact fluorescent grows light and incandescent light. Most of these models may not last long and are dangerous if water comes in contact with their bulbs. I recommend lights featuring high-pressure sodium or metal halide bulbs:

I. High-Pressure Sodium

A high-pressure sodium (HPS) bulb has a yellow glow that isn't as visually pleasing as the blue light metal halide produce. The bulbs can last for twenty-four thousand hours (about five years). HPS bulbs are suggested for greenhouses with enough lighting but want to produce more flowering plants, fruits, or vegetables.

II. Metal Halide

Metal halide bulbs emit a blue tint that mimics real sunlight and can last for twenty thousand hours. Plants become fuller when placed under a metal halide bulb. If you want to elongate daytime growing hours, the ideal option is the metal halide system as you can turn the light on before sunset and again a few hours after sunset.

5. Heat Mats: A heat mat will be a useful propagation tool when propagating plants or starting seeds. Plug the waterproof rubber mat into an outlet to generate heat. The heat will produce warm seedling trays that will help to grow plants faster.

6. Plant Hangers: To take advantage of all the available space within your greenhouse, plant hangers will help just in achieving that. You can hang orchid boxes along with hanging flower baskets. You can also hang tomatoes pot if you wish. You can as well install multiple rods in your greenhouse to offer ample space, and hang many baskets from it for an ever-growing plant assortment.

Advanced Ventilation

Eave vents and ridge vents are a crucial part of any functioning greenhouse with a serviceable passive system of ventilation. When the air is not vented, it turns out to be stale, stagnant and gives room for diseases to breed. To avoid this scenario, you need to install eave vents and ridge vents in your greenhouse. Both systems work similarly but on different parts of the greenhouse. The two units are operable panels of glass-enclosed within a frame separate from the structural framework of the greenhouse. The vent will open by a motor that is dampness-resistance, or manually with the help of a rod operator. It will open to a specific direction and give room for air into the building. Both systems have screens that prevent debris and insects from gaining entrance to the greenhouse.

1. Ridge Vent: The ridge vent is essential for a greenhouse. Warm air upsurges and builds up at the top of the greenhouse. When you open the ridge vents, the warm air breaks out and fresh, cold air breaks in. The ridge vents will also enable air circulation. If there is light wind outside, it will get into the structure and help circulate the air, reducing the spread of diseases. If your greenhouse is in use of exhaust fan/intake louvers, the ridge vents will help in getting rid of hot air, so fresh air can go into the building.

2. Eave Vents: The eave vents are situated on the walls of the structure and would also open. And this allows fresh, cold air into the building. The air would spread through the room and reduce the temperature. It makes the house calmer and helps lessen the emergence of disease in greenhouse plants. You can also add rain sensors to the units so the when rain or snow hits the vents they close automatically. If you operate an environmental control system in your greenhouse, you can program the ridge vents into your specified system. Without aeration, your greenhouse would become a glass box filled with stagnant air.

Advance Watering Systems

The perfect methods of providing your plants with essential sustenance are watering systems. Watering with the hand can become time-consuming and tedious as your plant collection grows. An automated system of watering is well-suited for plants that require high humid environments. There are several available watering systems. For example, a misting system, that sprays a mist and makes the air to be saturated. The water drips are larger than the ones provided by a fogging system.

You can fit all the systems with different nozzle heads and utilize within the same greenhouse. There are various flow rates for different nozzles so that you can create poles-apart zones. You can use a larger flowing nozzle to make sure seedlings don't dry out, while a small amount of water might be perfect for mature plants. You can program all the systems to work on a timer to control the amount of water that reaches the plants

1. Drip Misting System: You can use drip misting system for slow release of water. This system is perfect if you travel frequently or you have busy schedules. This system is run in such a way that it provides constant water supply to individual plants. You can fill the tubes and rearrange the holes.

2. Riser Misting System: This system is programmed for utmost flexibility and is mobile. Therefore if you regularly change the layout of your greenhouse, riser misting system will be your best option. You can place this system anywhere on the bench and move to a different area whenever you like.

3. **Suspended Misting System**: These misting systems are lifted above the benches of the greenhouse to give room for unhindered bench space. In suspended misting system, you will directly insert the nozzles into the water source. The building runs the benches length and it's suspended from a jack chain which you can position at any height you prefer.

4. **Retractable Hose Reels**: Water is unavoidable in any greenhouse. If you don't use a system or watering can, then the next probable option is hose. Most gardeners are aware that hose can be bulky and occupy valuable space. When uses a hose holder, and the unit usually twists and folds under the hose weight. A retractable hose reel that is mounted to a wall or rafter will help prevent these. A simple tow of the entire length of the hose retracts unit will provide a neat appearance and prevent tripping hazards. The reel turns left and right, providing maneuverability all through the greenhouse. You can also mount these units outside a greenhouse by attaching them to a garage or home.

Greenhouse Shelving

Shelving options offer additional growing and storage space for any greenhouse type. You can attach a shelf to the rafters in front of glass windows or add it to a solid wall. If there is enough space, you stack shelving on a wall. You can use this shelving for any conventional or glazed building, as they are designed to go with the aesthetics of the environment. You can turn a bay window into a miniature greenhouse by adding shelving. Garden windows usually contain several shelves for growing plants.

Best materials for shelving:

Glass: Glass is conventionally used in garden windows since it gives room for the sun to get to the shelves, and provided that you use saucers under the plants, it requires a minimal level of glass cleaning. The glass shelves would be the perfect artistic match to the façade of the window.
Wood: Wood is another aesthetically attractive option for shelving. I recommend cedar or mahogany since they can endure humidity and moisture. Once you have stained the wood, it will look like a conventional English greenhouse. Using wooden shelves will reduce sun to lower shelves, which is best for shade-loving plants like orchids.
Metal: Metal is solid and allows for the flow of air into the plants bottom. The aluminum mesh is an excellent option for bonsai that usually demands the movement of air to thrive. Metal won't warp or rust and is a handy option for any greenhouse.
Polyethylene: Polyethylene is almost the same with metal shelving in form and benefits. The main variation is that the former is plastic with reprocessed substance. The polyethylene is black and covers dirt quickly, while metal shelving is silver.

Bench Shelving

The lower bench shelves for greenhouses are handy for plants that flourish in the shade or minimal sun conditions. These benches can be about eighteen inches deep and position beneath the existing greenhouse benches. Addition of the lower shelf increases the available growing space and provides added storage space for equipment and supplies.

Shelf Supports

The shelving supports could be either a decorative corner or a simple metal bar. Decorative corners are an ideal option when aesthetics matters. You can attach a metal bar from the above or beneath the shelf to create a hanging shelf. They are available in different forms that mimic the traditional structural design and English greenhouse.

GREENHOUSE IRRIGATION SYSTEMS

One of the main issues you will face with a greenhouse is keeping your plants watered. In hot weather, they can dry out very quickly, and this can cause problems such as leaf, flower or fruit drop, which you obviously want to avoid.

If your greenhouse is in your garden, it is easy enough to pop down and water it, but if it is at an allotment or you are on holiday, watering becomes much trickier, putting your harvest at risk.

In the hottest weather, and more so in hotter climates, you will need to water your plants 2 or 3 times a day to keep them healthy no matter how good your cooling system is! Although you can hand-water the plants in your greenhouse, this can soon get boring and difficult to keep up with. The best and most efficient way to water your plants is to invest in a greenhouse irrigation system. Which you choose will depend on the size of your greenhouse, what you are growing and whether or not you have electricity and water to hand.

If you are planning to irrigate your greenhouse, then the need to be sited near to water and/or electricity can heavily influence your choice of location.

There are plants that require more water than others, so depending on what you are growing, you may want to get an automatic irrigation system that can deliver differing quantities of water to different plants.

You also want a system that can grow with you as you put more plants in your greenhouse. At certain times within the season, you will have more plants in your greenhouse than at others, so your irrigation system needs to be able to support this extra demand.

You do need to be careful because any irrigation system introducing too much water to your greenhouse could make it too damp, which will encourage the growth of diseases. This is one reason why you need to have your drainage and ventilation right to prevent damage to your greenhouse ecosystem.

You typically have 2 choices about how to deliver water to your plants, either through spray heads or a drip system. The former will spray water over everything in your greenhouse. The downside of it is that it can encourage powdery mildew on certain plants, but the spray can help damp down your greenhouse. It can also be a bit hit and miss as to how much ends up in the soil of your plants. If you are growing in containers, then a spray system may not deliver water precisely enough.

Drip systems though will deliver water precisely to containers and give each container exactly the right amount of water, so no plant goes thirsty! The downside of most irrigation systems is that they require electricity, which can be difficult, expensive, or even impossible for some greenhouse owners to install. You can purchase solar-powered irrigation systems which will do the job, but they can struggle on duller days. The water will come into the greenhouse with piping, and correctly locating this is important. Hanging it from the ceiling and running it along the walls helps keep it out of the way and stops it from getting damaged. Running the piping along the floor is a recipe for disaster as you are bound to end up putting a container on it and damaging it!

You will need a water supply and ideally mains water, but you can run some irrigation systems from water butts. You will have to check regularly that the water butt has enough water in it, but it is still much easier than manually watering your plants!

Overhead Misters

If you grow mostly or all one type of plant, then an overhead watering method is a great choice because you can water all your plants evenly and easily. For larger greenhouses, this is a great system because it will water a large area quickly.
Its downside is that it is quite wasteful of water because the water goes everywhere in the greenhouse, not just into the containers where your plants are. Your plants end up getting a lot of water on their leaves. If they are over-crowded or ventilation is poor, then this can cause problems such as powdery mildew and make your plants more susceptible to disease.

Mat Irrigation

You can buy capillary matting, which works as an irrigation system for your plants. This is a special mat that is designed to draw up water which your plants then absorb through moisture wicks that go into the soil of your containers.
The mat is kept moist by a drip watering system, so you do not have to run water piping throughout your greenhouse. It can just go to strategic points where it feeds the capillary matting.
This is a relatively cheap method of irrigation and is very simple to install. The big advantage is that it is very efficient in its water use, and there is little risk of overwatering your plants!

Drip Tubing

This is special tubing that you run throughout your greenhouse. It has tubes attached to it that run to the roots of each container to supply water directly to the soil. The big advantage of most drip systems is that you can control the amount of water dripping into your plants. This means that plants that need more water can get it, and plants that need less don't get over-watered.
This is set to drip at a certain rate or to operate on a timer so it waters at regular intervals. It will depend on the type of system you buy as to whether it is constant or timed. Timed is by far the best as it allows greater control of the delivery of water, reducing the risks of over-watering.
This is a very water-efficient method of watering your greenhouse with minimal wastage. It can also be set up to be completely automatic, which reduces the time you spend managing your greenhouse.

With some of the more advanced drip watering systems, you have sensors in the ground that monitor moisture levels and turn on the water when the soil becomes too dry.

If you are growing directly in the soil, then the type of soil will influence your drip-rate. A heavy clay soil will take longer to absorb water, so it needs less water than a lighter soil because in clay, it will puddle and pool, which you want to avoid.

When you are growing a variety of plants, this is by far the best irrigation method because you can control the water each container receives.

Planning your drip watering system is relatively easy. You need to divide your greenhouse into an equal number of sections, and each area will hold plants with similar water requirements. Depending on the size of the greenhouse, you may need multiple irrigation systems, but most are easy to expand with additional piping.

Drip irrigation piping comes in either black polyethylene (PE) or polyvinyl chloride (PVC). These are cheap, easy to handle, and bendy when you need them to be.

PVC pipe is often used in supply and header lines as you can solvently bond connections and fittings. Polyethylene connections, though need to be clamped. PVC pipe is also more durable, being less sensitive to temperature fluctuations and sunlight, but it is more expensive to buy.

Polyethylene pipe is sensitive to high temperatures and will contract and expand. This means it can move out of position unless it is held in place.

Your main feeder piping may be 1-inch or 2-inch wide, but for lateral, emitter lines, ½-inch piping is sufficient. Each row of plants will have its own ½-inch line containing emitters. In smaller greenhouses, you can get away with one emitter line for every two rows when plants are spaced less than 18-20-inch apart.

There are some different types of emitters available. The perforated hose or porous pipe types are very common and emitter lines with holes. The water then seeps out of these holes. Most will deliver water at a rate of anywhere from ½ to 3 gallons an hour. The rate of delivery is changed by adjusting the water pressure.

Alternatively, you can get emitter valves which allow you to control the drip rate for each pot. Emitters are usually spaced between 24-inch and 36-inch along the main lateral lines.

Remember that you need to filter the water, particularly if it is coming out of a water butt. It will prevent any dirt from getting into the system and clogging the emitters. This is vital as it will ensure your irrigation system works without any problems.

Some irrigation systems will allow you to install a fertilizer injector. This is useful as you can get your irrigation system to feed your plants automatically! Depending on the system, this can be set to deliver liquid fertilizer constantly or at specified intervals. This, though, is typically found in more expensive systems, and you need to be very careful in your choice of liquid feed to prevent clogging up the system.

The key with drip irrigation systems is to apply a little water frequently to maintain the soil moisture levels. This is a very water-efficient system that is easy to expand and works no matter what plants you grow.

Most people who own a greenhouse and install an irrigation system will choose a drip watering system. They are easily available and very affordable though, as, with anything, you can spend more money and get more advanced systems.

CONTROLLING GREENHOUSES PESTS

A greenhouse is an excellent tool for keen gardeners. It offers a much-needed space for growing plants outside of the usual summer season. However, while sheltering your plants from the components, a greenhouse can also be prone to harboring diseases and pests that could wreck all your hard labor. Hence the need to be more proactive in giving your greenhouse plants the best possible protection. The following are the ways to protect your plants.

- **Maintain a Clean Greenhouse**

To prevent any kind of pest or disease, cleanliness is the priority. As part of your general maintenance, the ideal thing is to thoroughly empty and clean out your greenhouse once every year. It has to do with washing down the surfaces and windows, cleaning all the pots and hosing off the floors. Removing plant debris, weeding in and outside of the greenhouse, and reducing algae are also part of the greenhouse sanitation. You will have a fresh, bug-free start for growing each year by doing all these.

- **Examine Your Plants**

It is crucial to inspect all your plants before bringing them to the greenhouse to avoid spreading of bugs inside. Just as crops and flowers like the warmness of a greenhouse so do pests and they increase rapidly in the heat. Therefore, ensure to thoroughly scrutinize any new plants for signs of larvae or insects on the stem or leaves before taking them in.

- **Sterilize Your Tools**

A good number of gardeners will often use the same tools all around the garden, moving them around the lawn, compost heap, vegetable patch, flower beds, shed, and greenhouse. This implies that they can easily pick up bugs from the soil outdoors and infect the plants inside the building. So to be very cautious, you will want to give your trowels, spades, and other equipment a good clean after every use. Soaking them in soapy water will do well.

- **Eliminate Every Source of Standing Water**

Standing water is favorable to the increase of pests and diseases so ensure there is no source of stagnant water around and inside the greenhouse. Be it puddle or jug; get rid of every single source of water.

- **Isolate Your New Plants**

Your greenhouse might be free from pests, but new plants can turn out to be buggy. The new plants can infest your whole greenhouse with pests as soon as possible. To avoid this scenario, you may need to put your new plants in an isolation chamber until you confirm they're pest free. You may make use of an aquarium with tight-fitting cover if you do not have an isolation chamber.

- **Use Insect Barriers and Traps**

There is possibility that bugs will always make a way into your greenhouse. Use a simple greenhouse pests control products to catch them where they fly. Products such as wasp traps and hanging fly papers can also use spider spray at the entrance.

- **Use netting**

Greenhouses require proper aeration, and it is not ideal to seal them up absolutely to prevent pests from entering. But you could reduce the number of big flying insects that come in by hanging netting, open windows, or other vent points.

- **Move pots outside in the heat**

In the summer periods, a greenhouse will usually become hot and dry through the day. Taking plants in pots outside will help cool down the plants and cut down the buildup of spider mites on them. Spider mites multiply in numbers in warm climates, so the ideal thing is to keep the greenhouse aerated and also use a mister to keep the humidity up. If you are leaving the house for the day, it's ideal to douse the floor of your greenhouse with water, which would evaporate into the air through the rest of the day.

- **Use potting soil**

Often ordinary garden soil will be packed with a lot of insect eggs, creepy crawlies and other pests. Therefore, for the plants inside containers in the greenhouse, its best to use a good potting soil or compost for potting them. The soil should be rich in nutrients and sterilized free from diseases and pests to help grow.

- **Practice crop rotation**

If you plant directly into the ground in your greenhouses, obviously you will not have much better control over the spread of pests and diseases inside the soil. Crop rotation is a better way to combat this by growing different type of plant in the structure each year. It will discourage the building up of pests in the soil since the same plant usually promotes similar kinds of pests.

- **Freeze the pests**

This is an extreme measure which you can practice annually if you think your greenhouse is overwhelmed. In the winter period, open up all the windows and doors for one or two days to enable your greenhouse to reach a chilling point. Doing so the temperature will drop drastically, and any pests inside including their larvae and eggs will be destroyed. The plants will survive this as long as it is not chill for too long.

- **Use biological pest control**

Using biological control methods, you can combat many common greenhouse pests such as spider mites, whitefly, and vine weevil grubs. Every pest has their corresponding organism that you can purchase and bring to the area infested to feed on the bugs; this will put their population under control. When the pests are wiped out, the control organisms die out since there is no other food source for them, so do not be troubled about damaging your plants.

- **Use a Pest Control Agency**

In spite of your best efforts, you still notice the persistence of pests in your greenhouse. Hire a commercial pest control agency that employs an integrated management approach to pest-proof your greenhouse. These agencies are equipped with the know-how to manage greenhouse pests. They do everything from moisture control to rodent control, inspection, and sanitation. They have all the techniques and tools required to quickly identify and successfully get rid of pests and bugs from your greenhouse.

MAKING A BUSINESS OF YOUR GREENHOUSE

If you have a successful greenhouse that grows beautiful plants and flowers, why not consider making some money from your hobby? You might not have ever thought about your hobby as a profitable business, but if you have at least a little bit of extra time and patience, you can make quite a nice income from your greenhouse.

Find Your Niche

For any grower to be successful, they need to be aware of and be able to make use of current niches and trends in the growing market. The advantage of greenhouse growing is that you can have an extended season of growth that other more natural growers would not have. This means that you can grow special flowers, fruits, and veggies that would not normally be available to others much later in the year.

There is always a market for certain crops, especially when they begin to become out of season, so this creates an immediate cash crop for you to make money.

Special fall flowers such as Dwarf Snapdragons are much sought after by late fall, and typically only greenhouse growers can meet the demand that most retailers need. But along with extending the growing time for rare flowers and produce, you need to find out what kind of production makes the most money in finding your niche.

There are often enough best sellers in the market, such as tomatoes and jalapeno peppers, and the popular demand may vary based on your geographical area. As soon as you find your niche, you can begin to make a whole lot of money in the process.

Becoming a Business

One of the first things you should do before you start conducting business is to become a business. This means getting a business name, typically done through your county clerk's office. Most who start a small business use a Doing Business as or Assumed Name; this means that income from your business is the same as income from any other place. You add up your income, subtract your expenses, and report the final amount on your tax return at the end of the year.

Unless you plan on opening a retail flower store, you probably don't need to collect taxes from your customers as you would be considered a wholesaler. However, if your business grows and you're concerned about your need to collect taxes, you can probably quickly speak to a CPA over the phone and ask. Usually, applying for a tax ID is very easy and probably done at your county clerk's office as well.

These certificates—your Assumed Name and tax ID—are typically very affordable, usually less than twenty dollars each. Don't hesitate to call your county clerk's office first if you want to be sure your chosen business name isn't already taken or aren't sure which certificate is right for you. You can probably also check online as many counties have their website where you can run off the forms you need and can find out the charge. Once you have your business certificates, you can open a commercial checking account at just about any bank and may also want to check to see if you can reserve a website name that is at least close to your business name.

Important: When coming up with a business name, you can, of course, have it a bit whimsical; people often assume a greenhouse or flower shop has a bit of whimsy or creativity. Just make sure that it still sounds professional and is easy to remember and spell so that potential customers can remember it and find it again very easily. For instance, you might want to avoid "Debbie's Total Supply of Flowers and Plants from Her Own Greenhouse to Your Table" since it's incredibly long and wordy, but "Deb's Greenhouse and Flower Supply" is much easier to remember!

Finding Customers

So, how to find customers, and what type of items should you sell? Here are some things you want to consider.

First, make sure your gardening is reliable and that you can grow enough of an inventory regularly so that your customers won't be disappointed. Being able to produce one flowering lily plant is all well and good, but if you want actually to make money from your business, you're going to need to produce beautiful flowers regularly.

This will, of course, mean being very attentive to your greenhouse and your plants. No one wants to buy their flowers from someone who comes through with deliveries only when they can. Yes, you'll lose some flowers here and there and, of course, can't always count on how many flowers you can grow, but to be successful with your business, you're going to need to have a pretty reliable idea of what you can and cannot deliver.

Next, you'll need to consider what type of customers you can support with your inventory. Flower shops sometimes have their own greenhouse for their supply, and supermarkets may have a floral shop, but because of how many flowers they need, they may want to deal only with a large commercial greenhouse facility. However, there are many other possibilities when it comes to customers that you can support. For example:

- Do you have any mini markets or corner stores near your home that sell a small number of flowers? Even if you don't see them selling flowers now if you were to talk to the manager or owner of the store, you might be able to convince them to carry a small inventory.
- Restaurants sometimes want fresh flowers for their tables. You may be able to speak to a manager about providing carnations or other colorful blooms for their dining area or décor.
- Retirement communities also sometimes have fresh flowers on their dining tables; you may be able to provide these for them regularly.

- Businesses often give flowers to their employees on secretary's day or when someone has had a baby or other occasion. If you're priced cheaper than large, national florists, you may be able to provide for local businesses when the occasion calls for it.
- Weddings, of course, are big business for many florists. While you may not be ready to supply to very large weddings at a moment's notice, if you spread the word among your friends and relatives, you might find that someone you know is interested in working with you, especially if your costs are lower than national florists. Many brides today are looking to save money in any way they can, so they may be happy to simply choose from the flowers you have available.
- Your friends and family too may want to see what flowers you have available on special days and occasions. They may check with you for anniversaries, birthdays, and holidays.

Very often, getting the word out there among your friends and family and local businesses is all that's needed to get your first order, which in turn can lead to so many other orders down the road!

Some Important Considerations

Before you just run out and start talking to those retirement home managers and restaurant owners, consider some of the following points:

- **Consider getting a website even if you don't plan on selling online.** A website is a great marketing tool because potential customers will often bookmark your site and visit again when they're ready to purchase. A website address is often easier to remember than a phone number, so customers might visit your site looking for your actual contact information. Websites are usually very affordable if you just need a few pages with your contact info and a few photos of your product.
- **Most places that purchase flowers from you may expect some type of special packaging.** For example, that corner market might be interested in purchasing single blooms that they keep by the cash register for one-at-a-time purchases. However, these blooms are usually wrapped in cellophane and may have new ferns or baby's breath inside. Be prepared with these extra materials and for the wrapping involved; don't just show up with an armful of single blossoms.
- **Stores may also expect you to provide the large vase in which these flowers are kept near the register.** View this as a marketing opportunity; put a card with your business name and phone number or website address on the front of it.

- **Get to know the accessories you need for many of your products.** If you're going to provide bridal bouquets, you'll need the little handles they fit into. Boutonnieres for groomsmen usually are attached with a pin. That retirement community may also ask you to provide vases. Shop for wholesale items online so you can purchase these things very cheaply.
- **Take a flower arranging class if you're very dedicated to making this greenhouse into a successful business.** Putting together bouquets and arrangements is usually part art but part science. Sometimes certain colors or sizes of flowers are just too busy or may look overdone when used together. At the very least, study bouquets you see online and practice some on your own before trying to sell them to a customer.

Another thing you might want to consider about getting customers and selling is to have some marketing material available. At the very least, you should have professional business cards made up so that when you call upon potential customers, you have something you can leave with them, so they have your contact info handy.

You might also be able to make up a flyer or brochure with some featured products. If you can't do this on your own, you can easily hire someone with a marketing degree to do this for you; chances are you might even have a friend with some talent that can easily design some business cards or marketing material. Any nearby office supply center can probably print these things out for a very affordable price.

Calculate Your Profit Window

To be successful with your greenhouse, you need to assess just how profitable the enterprise will be. This means that you need to calculate your potential profit window in advance. First, you need to take into consideration how much money you will have to put into the greenhouse project. If it is just a small amount of money, you can set aside the small amount you may need; if it is a larger amount, you can then plan for that also. Once this has been established, you can then think about the types of plants you will be growing and approximately how much their valued worth on the market will be. After that, it's just a matter of basic calculation to find out how much profit you would be able to make at the end of the process. Keep close track of your expenses and earnings along the way so that you can make the best use of your produce.

CONCLUSION

Reenhouse is a must-have for any gardener. It has so many potential uses and makes your life so much easier than wonder how you ever managed without one. You can spend as much, or as little, money as you want on your greenhouse, it depends on your budget. However, what is important is that you choose the site and then prepare it properly. Doing so will reduce the amount of maintenance you need to do and extend the lifespan of your greenhouse.

Your greenhouse needs to be secure against the wind and any potential damage from the surroundings, think footballs and falling branches. Set up properly, it will be very low maintenance and an absolute pleasure to grow in.

You can extend your growing season, being able to start your seeds off earlier in the year and grow delicate crops longer into the cooler months. For anyone outside of the warmest areas, it is essential as it will make the difference when it comes to getting your crops to produce a viable harvest.

This book has tried to answer all of your potential questions and show you the many benefits of a greenhouse. With everything you have learned in this book, you will now be able to set up your greenhouse and manage it easily. It will reduce the amount of work you need to do and allow you to grow plants that would otherwise have been out of your reach.

You do have to remember that greenhouses come with their own potential set of problems. However, most of these can be avoided purely by ensuring there is suitable ventilation and air circulation. These two issues are by far the number one cause of problems within any glasshouse.

Pollination can be an issue, but leaving vents open will allow pollinating insects in, and, as you learned earlier, you can always pollinate your plants by hand.

It is vital that you either have a suitable irrigation system in your greenhouse or that you water your plants regularly. They will require daily watering on hotter days, particularly if they are in smaller containers. Lack of water causes leaf, flower, and fruit drop, which will impact your potential harvest.

If you are planning on putting a greenhouse in your garden or on your allotment, then I'd recommend you go and size it up. Look for a suitable space and measure it up to determine what size greenhouse you can put in. You may decide to start with a portable greenhouse or a hoop house, depending on the space and budget available to you.

Making decisions about the floor and foundation need to be made right at the start as these are very difficult and expensive to change later on. I wouldn't recommend growing directly in the soil as it will quickly become a burden and turn your greenhouse into a chore.

I will guarantee that in your first year, you will overcrowd your greenhouse in your excitement. By the second, you will want another greenhouse or a bigger one as you understand the benefits and how great a greenhouse is. I can see so many benefits, and after a couple of poor growing years, this will make a massive difference to my ability to produce the more delicate crops I like.

Owning a greenhouse is a lot of fun and full of potential. I would highly recommend you get one, as large as you can afford and fit in. You will enjoy it immensely as it allows you to grow successfully a wide variety of crops that you would otherwise have struggled to grow. These useful glasshouses are well worth the investment and will give you years of enjoyment and growing pleasure.

Printed by BoD™in Norderstedt, Germany